NOTEBOOK

RULED PAPER

THIS BOOK BELONGS TO:

Made in the USA
Monee, IL
27 April 2022

95494111R00069